CELEBRATING THE FAMILY NAME OF MAUNG

Celebrating the Family Name of Maung

Walter the Educator

Silent King Books
a WhichHead Entertainment Imprint

Copyright © 2024 by Walter the Educator

All rights reserved. No part of this book may be reproduced in any manner whatsoever without written permission except in the case of brief quotations embodied in critical articles and reviews.

First Printing, 2024

Disclaimer

This book is a literary work; the story is not about specific persons, locations, situations, and/or circumstances unless mentioned in a historical context. Any resemblance to real persons, locations, situations, and/or circumstances is coincidental. This book is for entertainment and informational purposes only. The author and publisher offer this information without warranties expressed or implied. No matter the grounds, neither the author nor the publisher will be accountable for any losses, injuries, or other damages caused by the reader's use of this book. The use of this book acknowledges an understanding and acceptance of this disclaimer.

Celebrating the Family Name of Maung is a memory book that belongs to the Celebrating Family Name Book Series by Walter the Educator. Collect them all and more books at WaltertheEducator.com

USE THE EXTRA SPACE TO DOCUMENT YOUR FAMILY MEMORIES THROUGHOUT THE YEARS

MAUNG

Maung, a name of strength untold,

A legacy forged in hearts so bold.

From verdant hills to oceans wide,

Its spirit endures, a source of pride.

Through winds of change, through skies so vast,

The Maung name echoes from the past.

A beacon bright, a guiding flame,

It carries the honor of its name.

In every step, in every deed,

The Maung name grows like a thriving seed.

With roots that anchor, firm and strong,

It weaves its story through every song.

Through times of peace, through battles won,

The Maung name shines beneath the sun.

A family bound by love and care,

With courage vast and hearts so rare.

From village paths to bustling streets,

The Maung name journeys, where wisdom meets.

It carries dreams of hope and grace,

A name that spans both time and space.

The tiger's roar, the eagle's flight,

Reflect the Maung name's fearless might.

A symbol of strength, a mark of pride,

Its essence flows like the endless tide.

In hands that build, in minds that strive,

The Maung name keeps its fire alive.

A heritage rich, a tale untold,

It shines with hues of silver and gold.

With every dawn, its story grows,

Through every challenge the Maung name shows.

Resilient, steadfast, bold and true,

It crafts the future from what it knew.

Through ancient lands and modern dreams,

The Maung name glistens in sunlit beams.

A family strong, a name renowned,

Its legacy forever sound.

So here we honor the name of Maung,

A tale of triumph, richly sung.

A timeless bond, a noble creed,

A name that fulfills every need.

ABOUT THE CREATOR

Walter the Educator is one of the pseudonyms for Walter Anderson. Formally educated in Chemistry, Business, and Education, he is an educator, an author, a diverse entrepreneur, and he is the son of a disabled war veteran. "Walter the Educator" shares his time between educating and creating. He holds interests and owns several creative projects that entertain, enlighten, enhance, and educate, hoping to inspire and motivate you. Follow, find new works, and stay up to date with Walter the Educator™

at WaltertheEducator.com

www.ingramcontent.com/pod-product-compliance
Lightning Source LLC
LaVergne TN
LVHW020135080526
838201LV00119B/3918